on a date *with* disappointment

on a date *with* disappointment

poems by

Najya Williams

Button Publishing Inc.
Minneapolis
2025

ON A DATE WITH DISAPPOINTMENT
POETRY
AUTHOR: Najya Williams
COVER DESIGN: Victoria Alvarez
AUTHOR PHOTOGRAPHY: Anudeeta Gautam

◇

ALL RIGHTS RESERVED

© 2025 by Najya Williams

button poetry

Published by Button Poetry
Minneapolis, MN 55418 | http://www.buttonpoetry.com

◇

Manufactured in the United States of America
PRINT ISBN: 978-1-63834-130-7
EBOOK ISBN: 978-1-63834-126-0

First printing

CONTENTS

1	life story #29
2	generational curse retold
3	Introducing...
6	conversations with myself
7	conversations ~~with myself~~ my abuser
8	first stake
9	life story #24
10	An ode to Black only – or first daughters in their 20s who live alone and have a therapist
12	epistle for adelphia asiya
13	good mo(u)rning
14	black woman vs. death in the U.S. Supreme Court (remote due to COVID-19), 2022
16	vanishing act
17	life story #23
18	mirror, mirror
19	eruption imminent
20	"take a chance on us"
21	ON MEN WITH INFERIORITY COMPLEXES WHO PURSUE FIRE-FORGED WOMEN: AN ABECEDARIAN
23	John 11:35 [Unrevised]
24	life story #17
25	for the suns who aren't allowed to stop shining: a pantoum
26	wine drunk
27	sweet tooth
29	from the rubble
30	life story #11
31	but the memories
32	What Couldn't Be Excised

33	All Praise to the Wolf Moon of 2023
34	A BLACK GIRL'S INCANTATION FOR FREEDOM AND LIBERATION
35	TO THE EIGHT-YEAR-OLD GIRL WHO NO LONGER WANTED TO BE EXCEPTIONAL
36	let this sestina be safe

41	UBUNTU
43	About the Author
45	Author Book Recommendations
49	Credits

on a date *with* disappointment

life story #29

God decides to visit her creation, so she births herself on a Sunday morning. God is met not with reverence — only disappointment. How dare they not know her name?

generational curse retold

Adam gave his rib to Eve,
but he had nothing left for the fruits
of his sacrifice and love.
So, he watched as we withered.

But he had nothing left for the fruits
born to flower this earth,
so he watched as we withered.
Instead of life, he stewarded over death.

Born to flower this earth,
Adam had the greatest potential. Yet
instead of life, he stewarded over death.
If only composting applied to relationships.

Adam had the greatest potential, yet
he couldn't see beyond his own scarcity.
If only composting applied to relationships,
the decay of his love would've nourished me.

He couldn't see beyond his own scarcity,
so I left him in search of my own abundance.
The decay of his love would've nourished me
in a world too far from this one.

So, I left him in search of my own abundance.
I chose myself in spite of myself.
In a world too far from this one,
he never truly stunted my growth.

I chose myself in spite of myself.
Now, our past can finally be laid to rest.
He never truly stunted my growth,
only taught me how to be more with less.

introducing...

She's the only one still awake when I leave for the night
And don't be confused or mistaken
She is not an extraterrestrial being
I named her solar system long before this world was born

And don't be confused or mistaken
She has her moments of humanity
I named her solar system long before this world was born
But she got some grit and salt and grime in her

She has her moments of humanity
Especially when it come to her tribe
But she got some grit and salt and grime in her
Violence ain't gotta be the answer, but it can be

Especially when it come to her tribe
She'll flip this whole universe on its head
Violence ain't gotta be the answer, but it can be
Don't forget to remember who the fuck she is

She'll flip this whole universe on its head
Even to save a single soul nobody else cares for
Don't forget to remember who the fuck she is
Her worth far exceeds the finest gold

Even to save a single soul nobody else cares for
There's no price too high for what lies in her heart
Her worth far exceeds the finest gold
Yet most don't even know how to find a lost art

There's no price too high for what lies in her heart
To rest under her ribcage is to lay in the bosom of God
Yet most don't even know how to find a lost art
After all, what light is able to survive in the dark?

To rest under her ribcage is to lay in the bosom of God
Priceless protection when the sky comes down
After all, what light is able to survive in the dark?
...She is the only one still awake.

conversations with myself

>this is your moment
>to win and behold
>the fruits of your labor!
>
>I'm so proud
>of how you've survived
>the impossible and the unthinkable.
>
>you are still soft
>and this is your superpower
>that will keep you flying high.
>
>don't doubt yourself.
>listen to the quiet
>knowing deep within your chest.
>
>the future is bright
>and filled with
>promises of your glory.
>
>I believe in you
>more than I
>count on my next breath.

conversations ~~with myself~~ my abuser

falling prey to your insecurities
and cowering and falling
is simply what you've always done.

that you keep trying
to rise above the fire
is quite laughable.

it's not surprising
that you've been caught
in the crosshairs of failure.

what have you conquered?
who are you to deserve anything?
when will you ever be enough?

the past is overflowing
with reminders that
you won't get further than this.

there will always be a limit
to how much I'm able to believe
in the gift you're supposed to be.

first stake

i thought this was
supposed to be a gift,
a moment to embrace
the widening of my hips and the bloom of chest. ain't this a sign that
womanhood has come to crown me? adorn me with enough space in
my body to hold life and beauty and fertility and blessing. but as i
stand here, with my tied hands around this prickly, wooden post, i am
nothing more than a spectacle of warning. this new body is not mine
to enjoy or find home within. i should become used to the indicting
gaze found in the faces of family and friends and strangers alike,
charging me with arson at a trial prepared for me long before
i left the past for this
present. on either side
of me, i can make out
the shape of my
mother and aunties
and sisterfriends and
woman cousins and
matriarchs standing
wearily at their own
stakes, recovering
from the last fire just to
hope they'll survive yet
another one. i realize
now the gravity of this
fate. here i was
believing this would be
the last stake i'd have
to endure when it is
only the first.

life story #24

Black girl born with an old soul full of molasses grew up to become a Black woman with baggage left behind generation after generation.

an ode to Black only or first daughters in their 20s who live alone and have a therapist

The kids nobody gotta worry about.
Mini mamas keeping the sibs in line —
absorb the baby's cries
'fore they wake the whole house.

The glue, the ones who hold shit together
with no effort or sweat.
Maybe a few sobs into their pillows
for all the bills they're not yet old enough
to erase from the family's pile of debt.

The chefs, who memorized kitchen cabinets —
"Flour goes in the top right,
Sugar on the bottom left,
salt above the stove."
Wrote the grocery list
before they were asked 'bout it
"Out of milk, eggs, luncheon meat,
the bread don't smell right, and
we don't got the peanut butter Daddy like."

They got all the chores done and homework, too,
uniforms already starch pressed for school.
Applied to 100 scholarships,
filled out FAFSA alone,
hoping to get one fair ride to somewhere good.
The ones who held down two jobs
Monday through Friday,
and three jobs every other Saturday,
flipping hard earned twenties
into midnight oil miracles.

They grinded so long and so hard,
even their dentist said it's time
to ease up on the wear down.

Because it takes fangs
to do what they've done,
but you can't rewind time
once the enamel's gone.

The daughters, now women, have their own.
Get to walk around naked
and salsa dance in the kitchen.
Laugh at all the "we don't have time
for the silly shit" they missed.
Eat irresponsibly and cater to all
the naive wonder inside of them.

Old habits die hard, though —
they find the altruism in their hobbies.
Donate old clothes and
volunteer to teach classes at the rec.
Try to go out and make friends,
only to end up fixin' them,
'til they're no longer needed or wanted in the end.

Finally got a therapist after all this time,
but have no idea what to do
with space this open and kind.
Other than asking the doc themselves:
"How are you feeling? I hope you've been fine."
Apologizing for their trauma going over time.
Rattling off their self-help homework
as if there will ever be a real finish line.

This is an ode to
these warriors and wonders,
these saviors and sacrifices,
these fresh-faced grown women
and exhausted little girls.
May this be your space
to be seen and always known.

epistle for adelphia[1] asiya[2]

The silence between us aches like a wound that has forgotten how to heal itself / its edges too ragged to ever fit together as beautiful as before / I never imagined that we would arrive here / on opposite sides of life / hoping to find a land of milk and honey without each other there. /

I keep asking myself what I could have done differently / to save the love we grew together through tragedy and triumph / failed loves and prestigious awards / familial wounds and ancestral reclamation / mental darkness and spiritual enlightenment / yet the only thing that could be changed was how much of the real me you were able to see. / What a scary conclusion I never wanted to make. /

You were a masterpiece I was proud to display in the gallery of my life / yet to you, I was just a mirror that only served you best in the darkness of your closet / while the world enjoyed the fruits of my hidden labor, / spent absorbing the worst of you and offering back what rays of magic I had left. / And there I remained / until the reflection of my light could no longer be ignored. /

I love you / despite all the ways you tried to destroy my ability / to hold that sacred feeling even for myself. / So instead of bringing these words to your doorstep / to torment you with this pain like I have since the end / I hide them in the crevices of my grief / and pray that God will find a way to make where this relationship once lived / a place where we can both finally thrive. //

---

1   Greek origin, "dearest sister"
2   Arabic origin, "sorrow, distressed"

good mo(u)rning

I was walking down the street,
cosplaying as my usual self,
when someone said
"Good mo(u)rning!" in passing.

How did they know
to praise me for sobs well done?
How did they know
where to uncover me in broad daylight?

How did they know
I am grief's understudy?

black woman vs. death in the U.S. Supreme Court (remote due to COVID-19), 2022

Plaintiff: black woman

it's been two years
of rising above

                                            this isn't what

I imagined life would be
a paradise — I stage my own escape

                                            but life don't

offer gentle warning ahead of the storm
instead it runs with a deranged accomplice

                      and it's me left to pick up the pieces;

I got stuck with somebody else's job
Everybody's life depend on me

                                      What do you propose

my broken body surrender further
there's nothing left

                                                Where are

the hooks to rest my spine on
only pain greets me when I wake

                                              I blame death.

For the weight of this suffering,
For what I had to become to survive this,

                                        I was told this was

how martyrs are made
how the badge of Black woman is earned

                                           I'm surprised

that I'm here to hold my tormenter to the fire
a weakling, an underdog, hysteric even

                                          but justice is
                      a happy ending I'll never know

after Tyehimba Jess' "leadbelly vs. lomax at the modern language association conference, 1934"

Defendant: death

                                      two years too many
                        of being hard ground on the fall

I signed up for

                        new beginnings seeded daily
                            in dirt ripe for the birthing

work, that way, at least

                    be comfort in impossible times
leave a peace of fruit behind to quell bellies

I only wanted to fill my own shoes

                      But this ain't work I can picket
               I'm left with the trail of empty caskets

I do

                  indebt myself to this dying cause
            yet there's always more I'm to sacrifice

the days off?

                            few and far in between
                      I can't keep dying this way

I blame myself.

          for being villain in a role I was chosen for,
       for rebuking the benefits of the pain I inflict.

a temporary vacancy

      I should be grateful for the constant work
with no benefits, hazard pay, mental stability

I haven't given up

despite the loops of quarantined isolation as
    a wrath, a destruction, the plague even

the opposite of what I want
but I'll settle if I can just rest.

vanishing act

Been touring with Barnum and 'nem for a while now juggling my needs and her needs and his needs and their needs the youngins to join the crew when time came for their spines to grow into final form I learned how to do my makeup from my kit cover the dark circles spent burning the midnight oil tryna figure how to do my makeup from my kit used to have a lot of family but most of them legends now, fables used to lure in the youngins to join the stage has been home my whole life used to have a lot of family but most of them legends now, fables used to lure in the youngins to join the stage has been home my whole life [spiral text — best effort] Close your eyes. Now open. see my final magic trick? better than before but I've run out of upgrades so I must resort to the last trick up my sleeve would you like to

life story #23

Black tornado fell from heaven...brought the whole damn kitchen sink with her. Even the sky could not contain her ferocity and fury.

mirror, mirror

Don't you see the power staring back at you?
Great oakwoods tremble and the Mississippi part at your feet –
there's nothing more to demand from self. Now's the time to be free.

Your shoulders slouch under the weight of overbearing demands,
but this is no way to live, 'specially when the pain and soothing
lie under your own hand.
Don't you see the power staring back at you?

Black don't crack, but spirits do.
Your porcelain bones will never withstand
the weight of this world, so
there's nothing more to demand from self. Now's the time to be free.

Building your own cage was a societal inheritance,
but the master key always blooms from deep within the family tree.
Don't you see the power staring back at you?

Rest your expectations down at the feet of your oppressors,
that yoke was never yours to carry.
It was only meant to choke the life from you.
There's nothing more to demand from self. Now's the time to be free.

What you're begging to unleash won't come before the relief.
Calm your weary mind, everything you've been waiting for…is.
Don't you see the power staring back at you?
There's nothing more to demand from self. Now's the time to be free.

eruption imminent

quiet for all this time,
i can no longer hold this lava
to scorch my insides
instead of yours.

"take a chance on us"

Every cell in my body begs me not to fall again,
in love or into the trap of sadism under disguise.
My heart dares to whistle out its love song,
hoping to remind my organs of how sweet it sounds
when intimacy is allowed to lay salve on our wounds.
Yet, my brain remembers what happened the last time it heard:

"take a chance on us"

Harm fundamentally transforms the fabric of our being
by making abstract art of the DNA strands tightly wound
down into miniature fortresses of protection from the past.
Each base a casualty that's gutted until only carnage remains,
and our spirits are no longer able to ignore the pain that persists.
So, for every horror we bear witness to, there is a portrait
stored within us, warning the present and future versions
of ourselves to beware of trusting what appears to be mundane, like:

"take a chance on us"

I was told the treatment for trauma is exposure —
allowing the wound to breathe and bleed and build
a thickened skin to withstand the irritation life has to offer,
returning to the scene of the incident and confronting the ghosts
who remained waiting to be acknowledged and allowed home.
This new day demands I finally respond to her question and I say yes:

"take a chance on us?"

on men with inferiority complexes
who pursue fire-forged women: an abecedarian

"Amend her," an informal slogan for those
    who are both awe-inspired and threatened by her
beauty, as it travels from one corner of the earth to the other,
    enticing the most stubborn
calla lilies to bloom in competition. It is not easy to behold a
Deity, Goddess, Titan, Crown as jeweled and precious as her,
especially when your roots are planted
    in the same bitter, weeded plot of insecurity.
Failure to reckon with the demons clinging to your foundation
    will poison her fruit,
gaping her womb open to vitriol unlike any other because
how can you suspect danger
    when it is the love of your life who delivers it?
I've met many of these men before,
    who once fancied me in all my glory,
just to strike me down with the blow
    of a golden glove fist day in and day out.
Keeping me was no honor for them,
    but a flag atop Misogyny Mountain that proudly states:
"Look at what I can conquer! Look at what I can destroy!
    Look at what I changed forever!"
Morsels of my body – our bodies – sit
    between their teeth and rot until
no piece is recognizable as self, theirs, mine, other, safe, unsafe.
Only when bones are exposed does the world realize
    the damage has been done, that
protection is needed. But it is often already too late
    for the derailment to be stopped.
Questions fly into the air: What? When? Where? Why? How?
Reminds us women who've been to hell and back
    that no cares to treat the burns,
'stead they'd rather focus on what we've done
    to earn the affliction in the first place.

Tradition tells us that boys will be boys
        and to be big, we must be molded small
until our footprints along a hot-coal path
        only serve to pave the road for our men.
Visioning a new future is not a forgiving task,
        but I persist anyways. For
what will I tell my daughters and granddaughters
        when I lay this world in their hands?

"Xenograft this fortitude into the fabric of your DNA —
        you will always have what you need.
Yell into the heavens that any man who wants
        to behold you must call you by name:
Zelena, Goddess who offers light just as easily as she can remove it."

John 11:35 [unrevised]

[35]Jesus wept for the niggas for the girls for the gays for the kids for the people who were tossed discarded abused sabotaged silenced starved murdered buried and cast aside before their time into the sea of forgetfulness left at the altar as unworthy sacrifices for the vultures to pick bone clean sundried under the scorch of society's gaze broken by the inheritance of inequity driven away from the land overflowing with milk and honey squeezed bloodless into the ink preserving the holy commandments shaved down palatable for ghouls to swallow whole in the hell that has overrun earth. Jesus wept for Lazurus and for London Starr and for Bianca Davenport and for Diamond Jackson-McDonald and for Tyre Nichols and for Micheal Corey Jenkins and for Eddie Terrrell Parker and for sex workers shunned by their employers and for our incarcerated loved one who's been inside for twenty years and for our collective trauma that keeps growing and for what the state of existence has been reduced to and for the tear ducts that can no longer produce fluid and for the brain that is required to hold these morbid memories and for the inner children who refuse to face another disappointment in daring to have hope.

life story #17

Black girl born fire and brimstone. Skin hot with the world's anger — she diffused it with kindness.

for the suns who aren't allowed to stop shining: a pantoum

What is the sun if it doesn't shine?
Free.
A battlecry for liberation.
The foundation of a new world.

Free.
A refreshing quench for rest-thirsty lips,
the foundation of a new world.
If only you dare to believe.

A refreshing quench for rest-thirsty lips,
this is the revolution y'all been praying for —
if only you dare to believe.
Sometimes, the gift can only be seen in the dark.

This is the revolution y'all been praying for —
do not weep for me.
Sometimes, the gift can only be seen in the dark.
I'm no stranger to the shadows — they're my only place for rest.

Do not weep for me.
Learn to embrace the chill in your bones.
I'm no stranger to the shadows — they're my only place for rest.
Now, watch your worries shrivel in the cold air.

Learn to embrace the chill in your bones.
A first step in your rebirthing.
Now, watch your worries shrivel in the cold air.
[Hm.] Now, what is the sun if it doesn't shine?

wine drunk

And the moment these hands touched these knees
I knew my spine caught your tongue
Don't be afraid that these hips will kill you
I only take breath when I feel inclined to

I knew my spine caught your tongue
How I wound you up and spun it down
I only take breath when I feel inclined to
Cherish what I've left of myself, for you to hold

How I wound you up and spun it down
You'd think I've taken lessons on how to
Cherish what I've left of myself, for you to hold
And dance like none of me ever left

You'd think I've taken lessons on how to
Drown you with just one drop of wine
And dance like none of me ever left
Baby I was simply born for this

Drown you with just one drop of wine
The drunkenness of your lips color you sober
Baby I was simply born for this
This ain't nothing to play with

The drunkenness of your lips color you sober
Still trying to work out how I worked you out
This ain't nothing to play with
'Cuz the moment these hands touch these knees…

sweet tooth

He must've had some kind of sweet tooth.
To walk right up to me
and stare like there was no one else in the room.
Enchanted.
That's what I'd call him.
Enthralled. Engaged.
Somehow caught up in a rapture even Anita can't coach him out of.
He was savory and savoring this moment to encounter me.
And I let him.
After all, he is standing in front of divinity.
His gaze is the very least he should offer me.

But like most men,
he wanted not to admire me but consume me.
Ingest me with the rest of his treasured delicacies.
I laugh because normally,
I broadcast a warning.
A flare of "do not try me, you're not ready."
"Not for consumption, overdose deadly."
But this time I don't.
I allow myself to become another part
of his candied collection of baked confections and...

He soon learns a hard lesson.
That I'm not something he'll easily forget.
Every cavity,
I carve out with extreme precision.
Every tooth,
I chisel my way down into the pulp of them,
the pulp of him.
I'm inside of him.

Working my way through every vein sustaining him.
I'm sure this wasn't the sugar high
he expected when he approached me.
I'm sure this wasn't the kind of jaw breaking
he craved when he met me.
I'm sure this wasn't the kind of girl
he hoped for when he kept me
in his little
glass tower
fantasy.

I finally understand why he calls me a
snack, candy, his sweet thing.
He saw a cheap fix to his expensive thrills.
A geyser of joy at the top of misery hills.
A fleeting gift that won't linger,
that won't question,
that won't disrupt.

But he was wrong.
He is wrong.
He can't brush me away or floss me out.
The pain won't stop the truth of me from living in his mouth.
It will persist and so will I.
They say tooth pain is the worst you can experience.
I say it's the worst when it's self-inflicted.
He could've avoided this,
could've come out on top of this.
But he didn't know I was made to stick,
made to pick,
made to trick him into thinking there's a simple fix.

He must've had some kind of sweet tooth.
To do what others no longer dare to.
I laugh because normally
I offer a warning.
This time I don't.

from the rubble

What could we possibly recover from the rubble of our love
beyond the shards of our broken hearts and spirits?
Perhaps enough material to ignite a new flame...

Sometimes I daydream about the trust I held in you,
but the lightning bolts that spark through my chest beg the question:
What could we possibly recover from the rubble of our love?

At night, sleep makes a deceitful exchange with memories of you,
until I am left raw and open and hoping that there will be,
perhaps, enough material to ignite a new flame...

I saw you on the train last week, taking what used to be our commute.
Only now, the hand you hold is hers, in the place that used to be mine.
What could we possibly recover from the rubble of our love?

Yet I remain in wait, yearning for our souls to connect
where our bodies erode until we hold,
perhaps, enough material to ignite a new flame...

I've been told that faith is belief in the unseen,
and that God is the bridge between the possible
and impossible, so I ask Him:
What could we possibly recover from the rubble of our love?
"Perhaps enough material to ignite a new flame..."

life story #11

Black woman shed skin to save herself — she is finally free.

but the memories

The scars may never heal — fully, at least.
Dirt and grime sometimes bring them to life,
but the memories have long scabbed over.

There are faint pieces of my flesh under your nails.
Jagged, rough, as if they tried to clutch
to the rest of me before your theft.
The scars may never heal — fully at least.

Makeup works wonders to hide the
abstract art you've painted my self-esteem.
Even the world no longer remembers when I was your hero,
but the memories have long scabbed over.

I was taught self-sacrifice was an act of love,
but no one told me how ugly my remains would be.
The scars may never heal — fully at least.

I never required you to consider me,
and that's left you unaware of just how much you've gutted me.
But the memories have long scabbed over.

Apparently, you've uncovered more of my grace to exploit,
as if there's enough of my flesh still alive for me to offer you.
The scars may never heal — fully at least.

Healthy and whole and bouncing, what pain have you faced?
All I have to show for is you, the outcome of my suffering,
but the memories have long scabbed over.

One day, I may find a way to forgive your greed.
Or sooner, I'll find a way to be free from your needs.
The scars may never heal — fully at least.

But the memories have long scabbed over.

what couldn't be excised

And despite the war waged on our bodies —
    the chains slicing into the flesh of wrists,
    the collars bruising the trunk of ancestral trees,
    the brands defacing what God called holy,
    the ships splintering into wearied souls,
    the oceans making morgue of her floors,
    the auction blocks selling property dressed as human,
    the masters dressing sadomasochism as evangelism,
    the whip creating ruins of historic architecture,
    the fields sucking nectar from sacrificial flowers,
    the language stolen from excised tongues,
    the hope draining into the rice paddies,
    the freedom hiding in the shadow of the whipping post,
    the dreams painting unreachable heavens in the stars,
— we remained.

all praise to the Wolf Moon[3] of 2023

the wolves sharpened their fangs and claws
in preparation for the slaughter that would fatten
their backs and hind legs and bellies so they'd brave
the biting chill of winter's harsh judgment against them.

i watched them murder one of our own this fall,
laugh in our faces with blood staining their muzzles
and flesh still crying out for mercy on their breath.
but tonight, i only hear their grief stricken wails into the sky.

the ancestors provided us deer[4] with extra strength in our legs,
improved camouflage along the stripes of our fur coats.
we are not an easy target to capture now that we've gathered —
the wolves no longer lord over their favorite consumption option.

all praise to the wolf moon that starves our predators
into the knowing of our routine oppression and suffering!
may the feasting tables wither and hunting tools serve no use.
may their bellies' outcry make a joyful noise to those we've lost.

all praise to the wolf moon that enacts justice when we are unable
to quell the tyranny threatening to make us extinct forever!
may the cold remain a partner in this resistance.
may the wolf moon serve as a symbol of our defiant existence.

---

3   "Wolf Moon" is the name for the January full moon, as identified by the Indigenous peoples of the Algonquin Nation. This name was born from the hunger wolves begin to experience during the middle of the winter season. As a result, wolves often howl and shed their fear to search for food in closer proximity to human settlements.

4   Synonyms for "deer": ungulate, hooved animals, fawns, Black folks, Indigenous folks, brown folks, oppressed folks, marginalized folks, silenced folks, martyred folks, abused folks, queer folks, victimized folks

a Black girl's incantation for freedom and liberation

recite with caution

the beast of oppression
that packed us into a damsel tower
has started to salivate and grumble,
for our souls it plans to devour.

time has long abandoned us
smoke billows darken the air
our spirits are weighed down with soot
and the world doesn't care.

today, I stand before you
with nothing but faith in my heart
that You will raise a hand
to cast light through the dark.

we are desperate for a miracle
a sign that our hope isn't in vain
that one day the future will be ours
to mold and dream of once again.

as we close our eyes tonight
the truth has been revealed to me
that from every corner of this Earth,
we will be declared free.

thank You in advance for this gift
and the strength to overcome
to soon realize, in full body and mind,
that this battle has already been won.

to the eight-year-old girl
who no longer wanted to be exceptional

I understand why you rebuke your gift,
this cursed light of greatness that follows
no matter the day, hour or season.
It glows on your back like its own bullseye,
making an unmistakable target for bullies,
and their parents, and your educators, alike,
to continuously poke and prod until you
explode your power into the palm of their hands.

You don't know this yet, but when you get older,
you'll spend the rest of your life struggling to hold
the weight of your talent in its full force after suffocating
it for so long. You will wonder if it was ever meant for
your body and spirit to hold, but sweet girl, there
was no one else that this moment was made for.
You will need the magic that flows from your fingertips
sooner than you think, and you won't have the option
to shy away from it, so I need you to listen closely.

Stand. Stand tall and proud in who you are.
The children and adults around you aren't
ready to behold the deity that has come down
to claim her earth — they know not who they
lose. But sure as the sun rises each day, you
will touch the sky and shine as the greatest star
in the galaxy, warming the hardened hearts of a
world crying out for a tender healing and hope.
Believe in yourself, baby girl, even if no one else
does. You are the answer you seek — the force you
need. You have already triumphed. Now act like it

let this sestina be safe

With each news update about the state of our current existence,
I want to follow the chorus of voices that say it's time to leave.
But for the Black and woman and unyielding,
the world will choose to stoke the flames of destruction, together,
in the name of preserving a prehistoric, heirloom hatred.
Where on Earth could she possibly be safe?

Perhaps I'm naive to think there is such thing as safe,
that my basic human needs should extend beyond mere existence.
How dare I desire to live free from the pollution of hatred?
Who am I kidding — I will never be free enough to truly leave.
My sisters and I will gather our sorrows and burn them together,
until our tears billow into thick, Black smoke — unyielding.

I can hear the matriarchal voice inside telling me to be unyielding,
to repurpose my defeat into the materials I need
to construct my own safe.
So I vow not to daydream about the day
this burden and I won't be together.
Instead, my heart drums a soft beat to my resistance – existence,
until I am not the entity being forced to submit and leave.
There is no other option — it can't stay here [hatred].

Camouflage is insufficient, for it's harder to not notice hatred.
The painful memories of its volatility are unyielding.
I've bent beyond my capacity — it is who must leave.
Every storm must cease, so the vulnerable can finally breathe safe.
Retreat to the pits of self-perceived inferiority
from which bore its existence.
I am not alone — the voices of the oppressed
will drown it out altogether.

When the melody of our battle cry and righteous fear marry together,
the sun of our ancestors illuminates our toughened skin.
To be without hatred
is just the first step. We must also make a commitment
to unabashed existence.
It is time to exchange the uncertainty
weighing us down for an unyielding
spirit. Once our roots have clenched fist into the ground,
we will remain — safe.
Though the branches bend, I will not break.
It will take more to force me to leave.

Laying in bed now, I chuckle at my initial eagerness to up and leave.
I hear the rustle of my foremothers' steps guiding me.
We're in this together.
The path was already carved —
I've always had what was needed to stay safe.
Fear almost overshadowed how my power eclipses society's hatred.
Here I am - still. Nourished by a determination that is unyielding
and unafraid. My legacy will not be erased,
and neither will my existence.

The battle was well fought and almost won, but hatred
is no match for she who is Black and woman and unyielding.
She has claimed her victory, and ultimately, cemented her existence.

button poetry

UBUNTU

"I am because you are."

To God and the ancestors for provision, blessings, and guidance. I lovingly offer this project back to You.

To Mama for being a devoted friend, teacher, editor, coach, cheerleader, audience, and momager day in and day out. There isn't a version of me who would be able to do this work without you by my side. Love is truly insufficient of a word to describe what I feel so instead, I'll say: usy.

To Lex, Amari Grey, Carlynn, Kelcee, Chelsea, Brookie, and my entire chosen family for always speaking life into me and my art and offering unconditional investment so that I can chase after my passions. My heart holds the purest place for you.

To Christopher Thomas, my mentor, for being an unwavering ear of support and an endless fountain of writing prompts that inspired many of the poems in this collection. I remain in awe of you, your talent and the ways in which you salt this Earth with your essence.

To Shahara Jackson, my mentor, for being a bridge and a light unto my path. I can only hope and pray to offer future generations a portion of what you've given me.

To A and T for holding me and my work in your arms in the midst of COVID quarantine, post-graduate adulting, and our wildly chaotic schedules. May we continue to sow our words and wonders side by side in the years to come.

To the Obsidian Foundation Retreat (UK), Sundress Academy for the Arts Firefly Farms Retreat (Tennessee), Rutgers Poets and Scholars Summer Writing Retreat (New Jersey), and the Southern Esesu Endeavor for the fertile ground and safe environment you cultivated to nourish my writing.

To my Philly sisters and siblings of consenSIS and the Colored Girls Museum for the ways you've unknowingly held me in loving, creative space when I needed it most.

To Tanesha, Charley, and the entire Button Poetry team for believing in my words and making this Black woman's dream come true in rallying behind this project.

To Porsha Olayiwola, the Roxbury Poetry Festival team, and every person who made the 2023 Publisher Slam possible. It remains an honor to have shared the stage with such incredible talents.

To my mentees and students for the ways you've molded me into a better writer, educator, and human being.

To every person who has supported me for the last 10+ years and every life experience that has brought me to this moment.

ABOUT THE AUTHOR

Najya A. Williams (she/her) is a multidisciplinary artist who floats along the U.S. East Coast. She graduated from Harvard College and is a 2025 M.D. and Narrative Medicine Program Graduate from the Lewis Katz School of Medicine (Temple University).

Najya is devoted to the liberation and healing of all oppressed peoples, and this passion is reflected in many of her projects, service efforts and literary works. Her poetry, essays, and other writings have been accepted and/or published by a number of organizations, including *POETRY Magazine*, *Black Youth Project* and *Healing Points*.

Currently, she is a Managing Editor for the *Katz Journal of Medicine*, Editor for *Querencia Press*, Poetry Faculty for Pocket MFA, and Board Member for *Girls Health Ed, Inc*. Her 2024 TEDx Dilworth Park talk, "The Pulsing in Our Spirits and Our Blood" is now available for public viewing via the national conference website.

Looking ahead, Najya hopes to continue inspiring full-body wellness across the world, one word and patient visit at a time.

AUTHOR BOOK RECOMMENDATIONS

Never Catch Me **by Darius Simpson**

Heavy like the rock David throws at the giant we call Goliath, *Never Catch Me* does not flinch or shy away from the reality of what it means to be Black, oppressed, and targeted. Every poem created a small spark in the depths of my belly until I was a raging fire of my own making, ready to sear myself free from the shackles placed upon me at birth. Simpson says fittingly: "there's fires to start", and with the finesse and wisdom of a thousand ancestors, this collection does just that.

Crown Noble by Bianca Phipps

Crown Noble is both the wound and the salve to be laid within it. Phipps confronts the intimate breaks and kinks within her DNA that have brought her and her family into this moment. In doing so, she invites her reader to do the same, and ultimately, pursue a transformative healing that will persist for generations to come.

CREDITS

ASSISTANT EDITOR
Isabelle Miller

BOOK PHOTOGRAPHY
Emily Van Cook

COVER AND INTERIOR DESIGN
Victoria Alvarez
Charley Eatchel

DISTRIBUTION
SCB Distributors

EBOOK PRODUCTION
Siva Ram Maganti

EDITOR
Charley Eatchel

PUBLISHER
Sam Van Cook

PUBLISHING OPERATIONS MANAGER
TaneshaNicole Kozler

PUBLISHING OPERATIONS ASSISTANT
Charley Eatchel

SOCIAL MEDIA AND MARKETING
Paloma Gomez
Catherine Guden
Eric Tu

OTHER BOOKS BY BUTTON POETRY

If you enjoyed this book, please consider checking out some of our others, below. Readers like you allow us to keep broadcasting and publishing. Thank you!

Natasha T. Miller, *Butcher*
Kevin Kantor, *Please Come Off-Book*
Ollie Schminkey, *Dead Dad Jokes*
Reagan Myers, *Afterwards*
L.E. Bowman, *What I Learned From the Trees*
Patrick Roche, *A Socially Acceptable Breakdown*
Rachel Wiley, *Revenge Body*
Ebony Stewart, *BloodFresh*
Ebony Stewart, *Home.Girl.Hood.*
Kyle Tran Myhre, *Not A Lot of Reasons to Sing, but Enough*
Steven Willis, *A Peculiar People*
Topaz Winters, *So, Stranger*
Darius Simpson, *Never Catch Me*
Blythe Baird, *Sweet, Young, & Worried*
Siaara Freeman, *Urbanshee*
Robert Wood Lynn, *How to Maintain Eye Contact*
Junious 'Jay' Ward, *Composition*
Usman Hameedi, *Staying Right Here*
Sean Patrick Mulroy, *Hated for the Gods*
Sierra DeMulder, *Ephemera*
Taylor Mali, *Poetry By Chance*
Matt Coonan, *Toy Gun*
Matt Mason, *Rock Stars*
Miya Coleman, *Cottonmouth*
Ty Chapman, *Tartarus*
Lara Coley, *ex traction*
DeShara Suggs-Joe, *If My Flowers Bloom*
Edythe Rodriguez, *We, the Spirits*
Ollie Schminkey, *Where I Dry the Flowers*
Topaz Winters, *Portrait of my Body as a Crime I'm Still Committing*
Zach Goldberg, *I'd Rather Be Destroyed*
Eric Sirota, *The Rent Eats First*
Neil Hilborn, *About Time*
Phil SaintDenisSanchez, *before & after our bodies*
Ebony Stewart, *WASH*
L.E. Bowman, *Shapeshifter*

Available at buttonpoetry.com/shop and more!

BUTTON POETRY BEST SELLERS

Neil Hilborn, *Our Numbered Days*
Hanif Abdurraqib, *The Crown Ain't Worth Much*
Olivia Gatwood, *New American Best Friend*
Sabrina Benaim, *Depression & Other Magic Tricks*
Melissa Lozada-Oliva, *peluda*
Rudy Francisco, *Helium*
Rachel Wiley, *Nothing Is Okay*
Neil Hilborn, *The Future*
Phil Kaye, *Date & Time*
Andrea Gibson, *Lord of the Butterflies*
Blythe Baird, *If My Body Could Speak*
Rudy Francisco, *I'll Fly Away*
Andrea Gibson, *You Better Be Lightning*
Rudy Francisco, *Excuse Me As I Kiss The Sky*

Available at buttonpoetry.com/shop and more!

FORTHCOMING FROM BUTTON POETRY

Jalen Eutsey, *Bubble Gum Stadium*
Meg Ford, *Wild/Hurt*
Jared Singer, *Forgotten Necessities*
Daniel Elias Galicia, *Still Desert*
Chelsea Guevara, *Cipota*
Hailey M. Tran, *an everyday occurrence*
FreeQuency, *On | (Un-)Becoming: Poems*

Available at buttonpoetry.com/shop and more!